Albert Einstein
Genius of the Twentieth Century

written by
Patricia Lakin

illustrated by
Alan and Lea Daniel

Aladdin
New York London Toronto Sydney

For my own beams of light: Lee, Aaron, and Benjahmin —P. L.

For our café comrades, Cathy and David —A. D. & L. D.

❦

ALADDIN PAPERBACKS

An imprint of Simon & Schuster Children's Publishing Division

1230 Avenue of the Americas

New York, NY 10020

Text copyright © 2005 by Patricia Lakin

Illustrations copyright © 2005 by Alan and Lea Daniel

Designed by Lisa Vega

The text of this book was set in CenturyOldst BT.

Manufactured in the United States of America

First Aladdin Paperbacks edition September 2005

8   10   9   7

The Library of Congress has cataloged this edition as follows:

Lakin, Patricia, 1944-

Albert Einstein : genius of the twentieth century / by Patricia Lakin ;

illustrated by Alan and Lea Daniel. — 1st Aladdin paperbacks ed.

p. cm. — (Ready-to-read)

ISBN 978-0-689-87034-7 (Aladdin pbk.)

ISBN 978-0-689-87035-4 (Aladdin library edition)

0213 LAK

1. Einstein, Albert, 1879-1955—Juvenile literature.

2. Physicists—Biography—Juvenile literature. I. Title. II. Series.

QC16.E5L25 2005

530'.092—dc22

2004017092

CHAPTER ONE
What's Wrong with Albert?

Here is a drawing of a photo of Albert Einstein on his seventy-second birthday.

Not many people expect an older man to stick out his tongue for a picture. And, certainly not if he is a world famous, Nobel Prize–winning physicist. But, for his whole life, doing the unexpected was exactly how Einstein behaved!

Albert was born in Ulm, Germany, in 1879. From the time of his birth Pauline and Hermann worried about their firstborn. Why wasn't their toddler talking? Was there something wrong with him?

Einstein said he remembered being a toddler. He knew how to talk. He was simply waiting to speak in complete sentences!

One family story backs up his claim. His parents prepared two-year-old Albert for the birth of his sibling. They told him he'd soon have a baby to play with. Albert must have thought a baby was a toy. When his sister, Maja, was born in 1881, Albert looked at her and said, "Yes, but where are its wheels?" That was quite an advanced sentence from such a young boy!

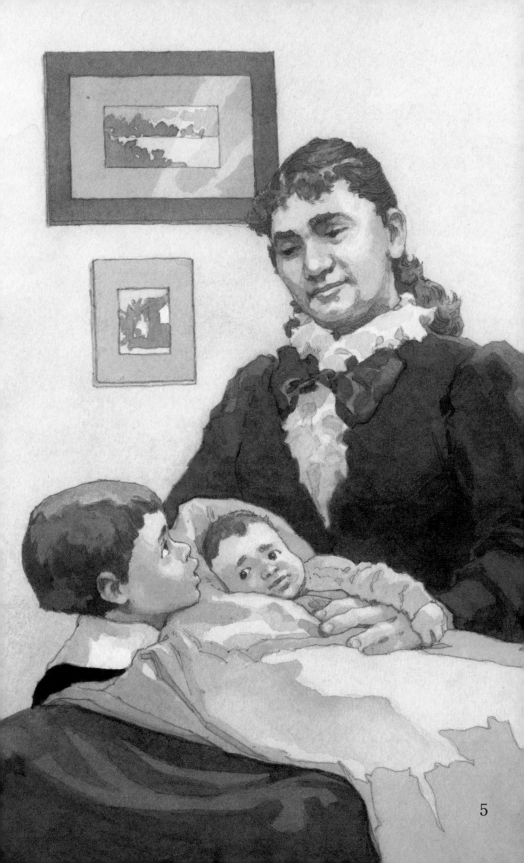

As a child Albert acted oddly when someone asked him a question. He mouthed the words to himself a few times. Then, after thinking about it, he slowly gave his answer. Some people thought Albert acted this way because he was "backward."

Mrs. Einstein may have felt that discipline would help him act in a more normal way. When Albert was five years old, she hired a tutor and a violin teacher for him.

But a simple gift from his father was what truly sparked Albert's mind and imagination. Hermann brought his five-year-old son a little compass. Albert was fascinated as he watched the moving needle. How did it know which way to turn? How could it move without being attached to anything? As an adult, Einstein said of that time, "This experience made a deep and lasting impression on me. Something deeply hidden had to be behind things."

9

CHAPTER TWO
A Different Kind of Student

When Albert was one, the family moved. They left the small town of Ulm for the city of Munich, Germany. Hermann joined his brother Jakob's plumbing business there.

When Albert was seven he went to school for the very first time. By now Albert's parents knew that he was clever. But his teachers and classmates didn't get to see his cleverness because they didn't get to know him. Albert stood apart, since he was the only Jewish child in his class. He was teased about his religion. Albert once said of those taunts, "They . . . confirm, even in a child, a lively sense of being an outsider." The boys in his class also ignored him because Albert didn't like sports. For his part, Albert didn't like his strict teachers or how they taught. They only wanted the class to recite facts back to them. Questioning the teachers was thought to be rude.

Albert's deep sense of wonder and his desire to learn were already on fire. Albert refused to let this school put out that fire. He rebelled! He paid attention only to the subjects that interested him, especially math and science. But even with his rebelling, he got good grades.

Luckily for Albert, his parents encouraged learning by reading, talking, and asking questions. And Albert had many sources for learning at home. Once a week his parents invited a medical student for dinner. This student became fast friends with twelve-year-old Albert. They spent hours sharing and talking about the latest popular science books.

Albert found many ways on his own to test his mind. Maja once watched him concentrating for hours. Albert was thinking about how to build a house with a deck of cards. She could never get hers higher than four stories.

After concentrating for a long time, Albert finally built his—fourteen stories high!

Albert's determination knew no bounds. When he first learned geometry, Albert took his book into his room. He spent the next three weeks reworking the book's math equations!

Albert liked to do "thought experiments." For these he linked his science knowledge with his imagination. When Albert was sixteen, he tried to imagine what it would be like to travel on a beam of light. He wondered: Could a human, or any object, go faster than that light beam?

CHAPTER THREE
Albert: A Total Failure?

As Albert's imagination grew his impatience with school grew as well. At the same time his teachers had finally had enough of his independent learning style. He was asked to leave school when he was fifteen years old. Albert was now a high school dropout!

His family no longer worried about their son's mental abilities. Now they worried about his future.

Hermann and Jakob's business was not doing well. The family had no extra money to help Albert in the years ahead. How would he support himself if he didn't finish school?

Albert took his family's worries seriously. He announced that he wanted to become a science teacher. He found an excellent school in Zurich, Switzerland, that would prepare him for that career.

He had to take an entrance exam. Albert was now a confident teenager. He didn't think he had to study, especially the subjects that bored him— French and biology. Albert flunked! He was shocked. He spent the next year working at his studies. He took the exam again and was accepted.

19

But even at this school Albert chose to learn in his own way. When he graduated, one of his teachers said, "You're a clever fellow, Einstein. But you have one fault. You won't let anyone tell you a thing."

Albert's strong need to do things his own way kept him from getting a job. He searched for several years. Once again his parents worried. Would their brilliant son ever find work?

With a friend's help Albert did! In 1902 he was hired by the patent office in Bern, Switzerland. New inventions were sent to this office.

Albert had to see if each one worked correctly. He loved this job. It also gave him time to work on his own scientific projects.

Albert's burning desire to know what was behind things was stronger than ever. His years of reading, his studies, his questions, and his thought experiments were the building blocks for some discoveries that turned out to be groundbreaking scientific work.

In 1905, when Albert was twenty-six, he published four articles in a famous German physics journal. Because of these articles many scientists now knew of Albert Einstein, the bright, young physicist who worked at the patent office.

CHAPTER FOUR
Three Famous Discoveries

PHOTONS

The first article published was about Albert's work with light. Building on the early work of another scientist, Albert found that nothing moves faster than light. And light always moves at the same speed, about 186,000 miles per second. At the time it was thought that light was just a wave. But Einstein found that light is also made up of tiny particles of energy. These particles are now called photons. His work helped future scientists invent the radio, television, remote controls, and CD players.

$$E = MC^2$$

In 1907 Albert's famous equation $E = mc^2$ was published.

The E equals energy, which is heat, light, or electricity. The m stands for mass. Mass is the stuff—or matter—that makes up all objects. The c stands for the speed of light.

Albert figured out that mass and energy are linked. If conditions are right, mass can be turned into energy. To do that, mass needs to be split apart. That will release the energy inside. But at that time scientists didn't know how to split up mass. Years later they figured it out. They split apart the tiniest bits that make up all matter, called atoms.

Albert's formula helped future scientists develop nuclear energy. Nuclear energy can be used to help power the world. Or, if made into a bomb, it can destroy it.

GENERAL THEORY OF RELATIVITY

Another of Albert's famous articles was about his general theory of relativity. It was published in 1916. For this work his thought experiments were important. They led him to huge discoveries of just how stars and planets move through space. He said that the mass of each planet makes a "dent" in the space around it. A heavy star, like the Sun, makes a big dent. A lighter planet, like Earth, makes a small dent. He reasoned that beams of sunlight and starlight in space are "bent" also.

Stern

Sonne

Es waire deshalb

↕ 0,84"

van grössten

Albert thought an eclipse would prove him right. In 1919 a solar eclipse occurred. Astronomers took photos of it. They measured the starlight peeking out from behind the sun. Those measurements proved that the starlight was "bent." Now the whole world knew that Albert's theory was correct!

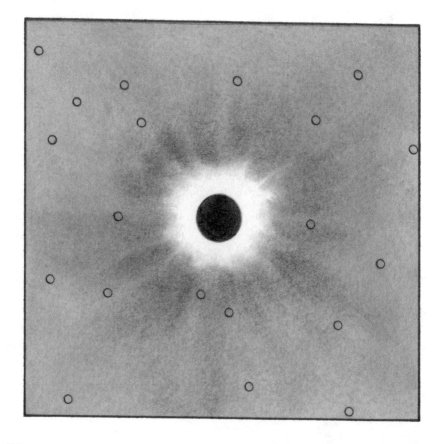

Newspapers from around the world carried the story. One headline read, SPACE CAUGHT BENDING. Overnight a star was born. But it wasn't one up in the sky. The star was Albert Einstein. He'd become an instant celebrity. He was hailed around the world as a genius. Few people, including scientists, understood Einstein's work. But they knew he'd made a gigantic discovery of just what was "behind things."

CHAPTER FIVE
Albert's Family Life

It wasn't just science that filled Albert's mind and heart. While he was a student in Zurich, he met a young woman named Mileva. She was a physics student too. They fell in love and married in 1903.

The following year their son Hans Albert was born. Eduard, their second child, was born six years later.

As Albert's family grew so did his achievements. He spent much of his time working and writing scientific papers. Mileva may have felt that Albert no longer cared for her. Their friends noticed them growing apart.

In 1909 Albert's successes meant he could leave the patent office. He was finally a science teacher! He was now called Professor Einstein and taught university students. But Albert's success didn't help his family life. He and Mileva were divorced in 1919. In that same year he married Elsa, his distant cousin.

It was also in that same year that his general theory of relativity was accepted as correct. Albert's fame brought him invitations. He was asked to be a guest professor at universities. He and Elsa traveled the world. But they made their home in Berlin, Germany, because Albert was a professor at the university there.

In 1922 Albert Einstein received one of the highest honors in the world, the Nobel Prize in physics. He won for his work in 1921 with light and light particles.

In spite of this prize and his fame, Albert Einstein's religion caused him problems once again. This time it wasn't simple teasing by schoolchildren. Anti-Jewish feelings in Germany had moved beyond teasing. In the early 1920s German Jews did not have the same rights and freedoms as other Germans. Albert spoke out against this treatment. During this same time Adolf Hitler, who openly hated Jews, was head of a German political party. In 1933 Hitler was elected to be the leader of Germany.

That same year Albert was visiting in the United States. He knew if he returned to Germany, his life would be in danger. Albert had been offered a job at Princeton University. There he could do research and work on his many scientific projects. He accepted the position. Albert and Elsa decided to make the United States their home.

CHAPTER SIX
Albert and the World

Once he moved to America, Albert had more than science projects to keep him busy. He spoke out against human cruelty in Hitler's Germany and other places. He spoke out for equality for all people. He spoke out for peaceful solutions, not war. Because of this Albert Einstein was now also world famous for his humanitarian views.

In 1935 Albert and Elsa bought a simple white house in Princeton, at 112 Mercer Street. But the world didn't need to know his address. He was so famous that a letter addressed to "Einstein, USA" would find its way to him.

Letters poured in from all over the world. Many schoolchildren wrote. Albert not only answered the letters, he saved them!

DEAR MR. EINSTEIN
I AM A LITTLE GIRL SIX YEARS OLD.
I SAW YOUR PICTURE IN THE PAPER.
I THINK YOU SHOULD HAVE YOUR HAIR CUT SO YOU CAN LOOK BETTER.
YOURS

Was there a special bond between this genius and the children of the world? Just what drew children to him?

Was it his kindly face and flyaway white hair?

Was it his famous forgetfulness? (He kept losing his house keys.)

Was it his way of dressing?

(He didn't wear socks because he hated when his socks sprung holes in the toes. But he did wear giant, fuzzy slippers.)

Was it his quirky ways?

(He stuck out his tongue for a photo.)

Or was it something more?

Albert Einstein believed in a child's power of imagination and sense of wonder. He also felt that his own imagination and sense of wonder were responsible for his success.

43

Albert Einstein died in 1955 at the age of seventy-six in Princeton, New Jersey.

Even today people think of Albert Einstein's successes as monumental.

His discoveries changed how we live. They changed how we have come to understand the world.

Albert was inspired by the workings of a tiny compass and went on to explain what was "behind" the universe.

He hoped that his work would help future scientists develop new answers to what is "behind things." Who knows? Maybe one of those future scientists is in elementary school today.

Here is a time line of Albert Einstein's life:

1879   Albert is born in Ulm, Germany, on March 14

1880   The Einsteins move to Munich, Germany

1881   Sister Maja is born on November 18

1885   Albert attends his first school

1894   Is asked to leave high school (Luitpold Gymnasium)

1895   Fails entrance exam for the Zurich polytechnic
       institute

1900   Graduates from the Zurich polytechnic institute

1902   Begins working at the patent office in Bern,
       Switzerland

1903   Marries Mileva

1904   Son Hans Albert is born

1905   Albert publishes four scientific papers

1909   Becomes a professor at the University of Zurich

1910   Second son, Eduard, is born

1916   Albert publishes his general theory of relativity

1919   Divorces Mileva and marries Elsa

1922   First visit to the United States. Receives the Nobel
       Prize in physics

1933   Leaves Germany and moves to Princeton, New Jersey

1936   Elsa dies

1940   Albert becomes a U.S. citizen

1948   Celebrates the creation of the Jewish State of Israel

1952   Is asked to be president of Israel but declines

1955   Albert dies on April 18

GLOSSARY

atom—the smallest particle of any substance

equation—a math sentence that states two equal parts (e.g., 2 + 2 = 4)

formula—a set of symbols that state a fact

geometry—the branch of math that deals with points, lines, and planes

nuclear energy—energy released when atoms are split apart

photon—a particle of light

physicist—an expert in the science of physics

physics—the science that deals with matter and energy

solar eclipse—a whole or partial blocking of the sun's rays when the moon passed between the sun and the earth

theory—a major idea that is based on observation

BIBLIOGRAPHY

Balibar, Françoise. *Einstein: Decoding the Universe.* New York: Harry N. Abrams, 2001.

Bodanis, David. *E = mc²: A Biography of the World's Most Famous Equation.* New York: Walker, 2000.

Brian, Denis. *Einstein: A Life.* New York: John Wiley and Sons, 1996.

Moring, Gary F. *The Complete Idiot's Guide to Understanding Einstein.* Indianapolis: Alpha Books, 2000.

Rosenkranz, Ze'ev. *The Einstein Scrapbook.* Baltimore: Johns Hopkins University Press, 2002.

Smith, P. D. *Einstein.* London: Haus Publishing, 2003.

WEB SITES OF INTEREST

www.albert-einstein.org

www.aip.org/history/einstein

www.pbs.org/wgbh/nova/einstein/index.html